Chaos in the Rose Garden

Monica Pastore

BookLeaf Publishing

Presentation by *BookLeaf Publishing*

Web: www.bookleafpub.com

E-mail: info@bookleafpub.com

ISBN: 978-93-95755-73-3

First edition 2022

For my Mom and Dad,

who, in the midst of my chaos,

never forget to water my roses.

ACKNOWLEDGEMENT

I wish to express my absolute gratitude to everyone at BookLeaf Publishing who was involved in bringing this poetry book to life. I can't thank them enough for organizing this writing challenge and giving writers like myself a chance. This was truly the most intimate yet, exposing experience I've ever had. I think poetry is the most vulnerable form of writing, so I found this to be both healing and revealing in the best way possible. So, thank you.

To my best friend Danya: Thank you for being my light in the dark. I will never be able to put into words how grateful I am to have you in my life. Thanks for reading all the books I tell you to read and for understanding every incoherent sentence I mumble.

To my sisters: Thank you for letting me be me.

To my brother Chewie: Thank you for existing. You are the most precious dog on our planet.

To my son Salem: Thank you for sleeping so peacefully behind my laptop while I cried and squealed as I wrote these poems. You are the black cat of my dreams. (I know you're secretly an exiled witch - don't worry, I'm working on breaking the curse.)

To my Mom and Dad: You're so good at being parents. I feel unworthy of you each and every day. Thank you for loving me the way you do. I love you more than life.

I would also like to send my thank you's to the night sky and all her stars for being the most consistent source of serenity and inspiration in my life.

Lastly, to the angels who send me messages through the clocks, thank you - I feel your love from the clouds, it's what keeps me going.

PREFACE

When people ask me what my biggest fear is, my answer is always the same: I'm not afraid of anything. Spiders are my friends. If I could live under water, I would. If you were to build me a house atop the highest cloud in the sky, I would forever be in your debt.

Fearless, I called myself… but it was a lie. I'm simply a master at pretending… though I'd be contradicting myself by saying that, considering there is truly nothing I value more than honesty.

So… a contradiction, that's what I am. Albeit, a self-aware contradiction, who, in the process of writing these poems, found her honest answer to the question: What is your biggest fear? Her new answer: herself.

I am biggest fear.

From a young age I learned how to perfect the immaculate to ensure I was a rose worthy of being picked in the garden. But as I grew older, I realized that perfection is a myth, and I spent years running to cross a finish line that does not exist.

To summarize the emotions brought forth by the truths I once refused to swallow, I spent twenty-one days rhyming words that hopefully have captured how chaotic it feels to be your own worst enemy, at the same time, you are your best friend.

I wrote these poems for anyone who feels like they gave everything, but it still wasn't enough.

I wrote these poems about all the feelings I wish I didn't have, as well as all the struggles I'm tired of hiding behind an illusion of perfection.

I wrote these poems to show the world how we can find beauty in the most chaotic of gardens, and to remind anyone who may have forgotten, or anyone who chooses to ignore, that the prettiest of roses can have the sharpest of thorns.

Pretty Can Be Torn

Every rose will grow a thorn.
Every cloud will start a storm.
Don't be fooled by what you see.
Pretty things can hide their torn.

Colours I No Longer See

Everyday is a different colour.
Calm yellows,
I can smile true.
Shallow blues,
I can swim through.
Until the rain falls and
washes every drop of colour away.
Now, every day is gray.
There is no colour.
My mind can't even imagine them.
Colours no longer exist.
Dark grays,
numb every emotion.
Pale grays,
hauntingly fog my vision.
This isn't me. And so,
just like the colours,
I disappear.
Until dawn surprises me
with a sun much warmer than
the one I was under yesterday.
A sun with scolding rays
that overwhelms the grays.
The rays stop the storm.
The rays end the rain.

And suddenly,
the colours come back.
But they look different.
And I'm too busy fearing
the gray cloud above me
to greet them.
I give all my attention
to the rain that has yet to fall
and thus, forget to enjoy
the colours around me.
Though I'm strong enough
to stand in the blues again,
my legs have weakened.
Though I can hear the calm yellows
knocking on my door,
I'm too afraid to answer.
Because I know
they won't look the same.
My days of colours have grown foreign.
It's not easy to recognize them.
Most days, I can't even
remember their names.
This cycle of colour loss
has blossomed a fear
I never thought I would have.
A fear that, sooner than later,
the shallow blues will grow deep
and drown me, and
the calm yellows will grow impatient

and walk away.
Tell me,
how will I find myself
when the entire rainbow
has turned gray?

3:33

5

Where are you now?
I think of you a lot.
Can you see me when I find
your messages on the clock?
I wish you were here to peel my clementines
and spread butter on my bread.
I wish you were still rocking in your chair
and watching me colour the roses red.
I wish you stayed with them a little longer
and then maybe we could've met.
I wish you could answer all of my questions.
I wish I had been older when you left.
Until we meet again above
I'll wear a watch wherever I go,
so the three of you can reach me
as I continue this life below.

Old Me

6

Dear Old Me,

I'm trying to find you,
I swear I am.
You're the same as holding water,
I'm left with empty hands.
I'm sorry I couldn't keep up with us.
Intuition says you can't be found.
You have a potential worthy of stars.
I'm so sorry I let you down.

Ice Dragon

She burns golden
from within
but nobody sees her fire.
She trained herself to hide it
and perfected
the art of a liar.

Born with a habit
of sabotaging her potential
and covering her glimmer
with used paint.
She destroyed the most
rare canvas of all
to fit the puzzle
of another's fate.

The last Ice Dragon.
Her frozen scales
follow the cycle of the moon.
Thawing only when she's whole
and just like Luna,
those nights are few.

They stole her warmth,
tracked it like the Sun's.

She fed them her heart,
they fed her half truths.
They took her kindness
for what it wasn't.
They consumed her fire
like the sweetest fruit.

The last Ice Dragon.
Her body too small
to cage the fire in her soul.
She's the most delicate,
mighty creature
who hides her magic
in fear of living
too bold.

And though she'll never say it,
since she knows
they won't understand,
all her days feel like
the end of a fairytale
about a single flame,
abandoned,
on a frozen land.

Dopamine War

Oh!
My dopamine is high today!
Now I see the sun for who she is.
I'm so grateful to live beneath her.
I feel unworthy of her light.
How did I forget how warm sun rays are?

Oh...
My dopamine is high today?
That's a gift I can't accept.
A hidden threat I can't ignore.
Truly, I loathe suiting up for battle,
yet I can't help but start the war.

Sky Nor Water

The tide can't take me under
if I learn to fly away.
The clouds can't blind my vision
if I take cover in the waves.
The sky stole my scales.
The water stole my wings.
I have a fin and a feather.
I am both and I am neither.
Born a mystical treasure.
Exiled a worthless creature.

Lost

How does one tell another
they are the equivalent to
the last car on the road
moments from the break of dawn,
stuck at a red light
with a tank near empty,
in silence,
if it weren't for
their left blinker... ?

There's Always Tomorrow

When I'm out of my element,
  I wish I weren't so delicate.
When I look in the mirror,
  I wish I weren't in fear.
When I'm certain I won't be alright,
  I wish the voices weren't louder at night.
When my darkness hides the light,
  I wish I could find the strength to fight.
When the moon guides a clear way,
  I wish I'd follow her, but I stay.
When the sun starts the day,
  I wish I wouldn't sleep it away.
But then the rain comes,
and it washes away my sorrows,
  which reminds me that
    there's always tomorrow.

Skeletons & Leaves

13

Skeltons strung up in the trees.
Kids drowning in the leaves.
I don't have a care anymore.
As long as the cider is warm when I get back.
Then I have something to look forward to.
The cider was cold.
I went to sleep early so I may wake at dawn
tomorrow.
If I do, I will sing you Good Morning.
I slept past noon.
Can you remember the last time the morning
was good?
I can't.
So, I'll ignore everyone.
Leave me to the skeletons and leaves.

The Smallest Circle, Please

A company of two is fine,
though, I prefer less.
Any more is crossing a line.
And I am tired
   of
      cleaning
    that
         mess.

To those who loved to watch
my petals burn

I convinced myself
that I was in love with your hatred,
as if I enjoyed setting fire
to the bed of roses
I spent all my life growing.

A pearls fate is the deep end,
a roses fate is death

No one warned me
how heavy pearls can get,
or how roses
are a pain to keep up with.

Does that make me pathetic?

I wear pearls, but I know the square root of pie,
so it's not hard to understand how this works.
How when a girl can't help but be desired,
the world will pretend she can't ever be hurt.

I'll admit, I played along.

Every morning, I'd step over the threshold
while I ran sweaty palms down my dress.
I'd pick the pinkest roses in my garden
to build a crown to hide my mess.

I showered in perfume to mask the smell of
denial.

Thorns burrowed deep in places I couldn't reach
without them seeing me tend to the wounds,

so I learned to hold the tears and ignore the pain.
My purpose lost to please the lot of you.

Deep breaths, alone, under the stars.

The moon became my safe haven.
I let her watch me cry in front of mirrors.
That's when I realized that they won.
That's when I became my biggest fear.

I locked myself in the garden.

If you need me, which I doubt you will,
I'll be watering the roses with the sharpest thorns.
I've dug myself a bed here,
it's quiet, and it's warm.

To fall asleep, I tell myself:

In a garden full of flowers
a rose is the last they'd pick.
This keeps me from growing curious
of what's going on outside the walls I built.

Don't come looking for me.

I put the pearls back where I found them,
hopefully, that makes it clear.
I don't want to be that girl again.
I just want to disappear.

Shapeshifter

18

I am a glass slipper that fits all.
I am a melody for every song.
I mastered the art of acting
to be the girl for everyone.

Bitter Sweet

You're laughing, the natural kind,
and you picked up after yourself today.
I'm telling you a story
and for once, you have something to say.
This is somewhere we can meet.
I love you when you're sweet.

I blinked wrong again,
and my words became prey.
How did I offend you?
Just let me walk away.
You scare me 'cause you're bigger.
I hate you when you're bitter.

Are the delights worth the violence?
The cycle of rage, guilt, and denial?

You win again I can't compete.
Your bitter side overpowers your sweet.

Shelf Life

You pushed my buttons,
so I laughed.
It made you smile.
I smiled back.

I watched you from afar.
Your friends adore you like the sun,
you make them sparkle like the stars.
Will you let me join your fun?

Oh, did you leave this here for me?
Was it you who left the ladder out?
I must show you the smile I'm now wearing.
Fearlessly, I'm climbing down.

I followed your laugh to find you,
and when I finally caught your eye
you looked at me in disbelief.
Do I look different when I'm not up high?

I made my way to sit beside you,
that's when your eyes lost all the lust.
You said, "You don't belong here.
You can't sit with us."

Growing Pains

I wonder what it must feel like,
to still look at the stars and dream.
I wish I still felt that magic touch,
the one that would fill every seam.

That feeling of so much to conquer,
like you might swim under water and breathe.
Or find a white rabbit who'll lead you home.
Or a mermaid calling you to her stream.

Is this the consequence of growing up,
the loss of all I thought I could be?
It's not easy to follow the dreams I had
when I can't find magic in this reality.

My purpose has been lost in the past.
I followed the wrong rabbit, it seems.
There are no magic stars here to wish on.
I can't dream.
        I can't feel.
            I can't breathe

I'm Fine

22

I'm my biggest enemy.
My mind plays all my future mistakes on repeat.
Forgot to eat breakfast, accidentally.
Ivy, the poison kind, has grown over my identity.
No one ever hears what I'm saying, even when
they're listening.
Everyday I find a way to sabotage my journey.

Chocolate Cake

Before I left, I hated chocolate cake.
Yet, I still made you one every October.
I lit all of your candles with my fire.
I thought you wished we'd last forever.
Blindly, I chose your comfort over mine.
I held your hand in every crowd.
But whenever I took the stage
you refused to help me down.
I would've rearranged the stars if you asked,
but my acts of love were never enough.
It took him two months to call you pretty
and in two seconds you were in love.
I miss you. It's been more than a year.
I've forgotten how to laugh.
I'm different now. I'm sure you are too.
I guess it's best we're in the past.
It's cancer season again.
I wonder if you remember my sign.
I regret not sending you a birthday text.
Do you regret not sending me mine?
My mom asked if I wanted a gift this year.
But she can't give what she can't take.
So, I shook my head as I watched the oven
burn my chocolate cake.

My Violet in the Attic

My heart is empty, it echoes.
As does the madhouse in my head.
Home to a ghost girl drawing circles.
She tells me: Stay put. Stay quiet. Stay cold.
There are days where she is the only thing I
know.
Weeks, even.
She draws my clocks. I lose time.
She locks away the parts of me they love.
Her nightmares flood my vision,
so nothing looks as it should.
She wraps my light in barbed wire
to keep the other girl from finding me.
The flower locked in the attic,
barren if it weren't for the small skylight
above a standing, cracked mirror.
I get glimpses of her a few times each month.
She still smiles when it rains.
She still feels the warmth of the sun.
She still loves her reflection.
Although she's grown silent as I've grown older,
occasionally, I still hear her whisper.
She tells me: Be patient. Be gentle. Be bold.
She grows fairy wings every full moon
and flies up to the sky light

to draw a heart around my name
on the frost covered glass.
She finds ways to fill my heart,
while Ghost Girl is busy cutting up my art.
Ghost Girl, my haunting master.
It scares me to admit
she's me as much as my blood is.
The flower in the attic, I'll call her Violet,
she's the one we all love to be with.
Violet once told me:
Be patient. Be gentle. Be bold.
So, I told myself that
one day:
I'll find my way through the madhouse.
I'll find the key to the attic door.
I'll open all the windows.
I'll hand wash every single floor.
Violet will plant us roses.
Ghost girl will make us lunch.
In peace, they'll coexist.
In the garden, they'll bury my chaos.

Who Am I?

An artist's soul
will deny their potential.
The soul of an artist
can never be full.
Too many colours.
Too many words.
Nonetheless,
I still climb the tree of destiny
with my ink and my pad in hand,
blank and ready.
It's the thoughts, you see,
they can't escape through
the feather I hold
when the storm in my head
is craving every untold.
Until they choose a path,
I won't want to wait, but I'll wait.
I'll keep waiting and wanting.
Wanting to wait.
Waiting to want.
And in time,
I will write as I climb.
And I will keep writing.
Because the day I found myself
was the moment I heard the voice

of a girl I thought dead.
She said, you will find purpose
through your writing. And so,
I promised myself,
I would write.
I told myself:
I am a daughter.
I am a sister.
I am a dreamer.
I am a writer.
I will write to live.
I will die to write.

www.ingramcontent.com/pod-product-compliance
Lightning Source LLC
Chambersburg PA
CBHW070723160726
48003CB00006BA/2352

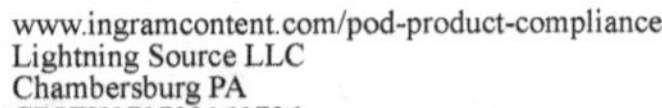
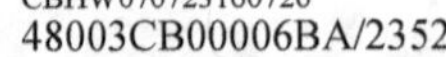